Hope Is an Arrow

THE STORY OF LEBANESE AMERICAN POET KAHLIL GIBRAN

CORY McCARTHY

ILLUSTRATED BY EKUA HOLMES

CANDLEWICK PRESS

There once was a boy shot from a bow like an arrow. Strong and straight, he flew across the world, connecting many people with the power of his words.

But not right away.

At first, he was Gibran Khalil Gibran, a small, shy boy who barely spoke and lived in a land of deep valleys, snowy mountains, and ancient trees.

Khalil loved his country, Lebanon, even though its people were like two headwinds crashing together. Christians swept all their strength in one direction, while the Druze gusted in the other.

Khalil's Maronite family was often in trouble, and he wished he knew what to do.

He escaped into the woods.

There the silence of the great cedar trees inspired him, and as he stared up into the branches that had held strong against many winds over thousands of years, he felt a secret hope bloom inside.

"Shall my heart become a tree heavy-laden with fruit that I may gather and give unto them?"

Someday soon, it would. But not yet.

On one climb through the woods, he fell off a cliff like an arrow shot all wrong.

He broke his shoulder, and his parents tied a wooden cross to his back to straighten his bones.

Khalil healed in silence and stillness, thinking, praying, dreaming. When people came to his home, his mother would look at him kindly, hold a finger to her lips, and say to the visitor, "Hush. He's not here."

Khalil listened as his people's great fear of one another turned into a terrible storm, and even his secret hope to spread love and understanding could not stop horrible things from happening.

Soon the Gibran family lost their home and everything they owned, and Khalil's father was sent to jail.

Khalil, his mother, and his three siblings could not stay in Lebanon anymore. They would take a ship to America.

Khalil was afraid to leave his home and father, but he reached inside and held on to his secret hope.

"The sea that calls all things unto her calls me, and I must embark."

First they crossed the Mediterranean Sea, the waves glowing with blue sunlight.

Next they sailed the deeper, darker Atlantic Ocean,
which murmured like a giant in its sleep.

Khalil's family arrived in Boston, a loud, crowded city where people spoke Arabic, English, and many more languages.

Khalil attended the Quincy School. He was placed in a special class for immigrant children, and his teachers shortened and changed his name.

Now when he looked in the mirror, he saw two boys: Kahlil Gibran, the Arab American, and Gibran Khalil Gibran, the Lebanese boy who missed his father and the snowy mountains of home.

"Deep is your longing for the land of your memories."

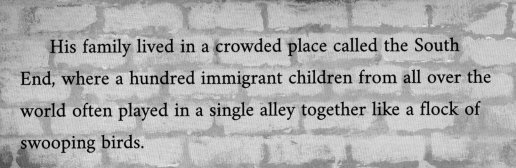

His family lived in a crowded place called the South End, where a hundred immigrant children from all over the world often played in a single alley together like a flock of swooping birds.

His mother saved enough money to open a family store by peddling goods, but her hard work was looked down upon by many people in America. Kahlil saw that Boston was as divided as Lebanon, only here, the wealthy crashed with the poor.

Kahlil watched his mother leave their house every day with a fifty-pound bag of linens and lace on her back. He was proud of how hard she worked, but not proud of how people spit at his family's differences. He wished he knew what to do.

"He only bent his head; and those who stood near saw his tears falling."

Kahlil knew deep down that his secret hope was the only way to best this great, mean-spirited fear of difference, but he couldn't find the words in English or Arabic.

So he began to draw.

His teachers saw something special in his pictures right away, and they sent him to a museum, where he met artists, including a photographer named Fred Holland Day, who took many photographs of Kahlil and helped him develop his art.

Kahlil's drawings became stronger and more enchanting. At first he gave them away to anyone who needed them. Then he sold his pictures to a publisher, who printed some of them on the covers of books.

Kahlil felt like this might be his moment to share his secret hope.

But his mother disagreed. She worried that too much success would change Kahlil's young heart. Like a stable bow, she shot her arrow of a son back to Lebanon, to study in the capital city, Beirut.

Beirut was bold, one of the oldest cities in the world. Kahlil studied hard and learned how to write in Arabic, but he felt that his classes were too religious, and his spirit rebelled.

Kahlil wanted to believe in all religions and all people.

"Alone and without his nest shall the eagle fly across the sun."

During the summers, he escaped to his old hometown in the mountains. There, beneath the great cedars that had held strong for thousands of years, he began to write.

"We are the seeds of the tenacious plant, and it is in our ripeness and our fullness of heart that we are given to the wind and are scattered."

Kahlil returned to Boston, ready to share his message.

As soon as he arrived, he learned that his sister had passed away. His brother departed next. And then he lost his mother. They all died from different illnesses.

Kahlil's sadness was like a wall between two gardens, but he still wanted to honor his family's lives with his secret hope.

"Know that all the blessed dead are standing about you and watching."

Kahlil began to write and draw more than ever.

He moved to the electric shining heart of America, New York City, and there his secret hope began to take a new shape.

A strong, straight arrow—one that would not be turned away by any wind.

He wrote poems to connect the people of Lebanon. And he wrote poems to help Americans come together in celebration of their many differences.

"Work is love made visible."

Kahlil's secret hope became a book called
The Prophet.

*"Let there be spaces in your togetherness,
And let the winds of the heavens dance
between you.
Love one another, but make not a
bond of love:
Let it rather be a moving sea between
the shores of your souls."*

Kahlil Gibran became an arrow shot true, an arrow made from the strength of Lebanese cedars and feathered by the spirit of American independence.

And right now—right now as you read this—his words still fly across the world, in more than forty different languages and through many crashing winds, to bring all who read them straight to the heart of hope.

SOURCE NOTES AND ADDITIONAL STORIES FROM KAHLIL GIBRAN'S LIFE

p. 3   a boy shot from a bow like an arrow
This phrase alludes to a line from *The Prophet* that is perhaps its most quoted line—and the one that sparked this biography: "You are the bows from which your children as living arrows are sent forth."

As a Lebanese American, my heart is alive with Gibran's words and art, and I wrote this book for my own little arrow of a son, to introduce him to the breathtaking life balance presented in *The Prophet* and encourage him to absorb Gibran's message: that love, understanding, and hope are choices we make every day.

p. 6   "*Shall my heart become a tree heavy-laden with fruit that I may gather and give unto them?*": Kahlil Gibran, 98.
Gibran was born in Bsharri, in what is now Lebanon, in 1883. Bsharri is located in a mountainous region next to the Forest of the Cedars of God (Horsh Arz el-Rab), a UNESCO World Heritage Site that is home to the only cedars in Lebanon to have survived Roman deforestation.

p. 9   "Hush. He's not here": quoted in Jean Gibran and Kahlil Gibran, 31.
Gibran described this repeated scene in a 1915 letter, saying that he felt his mother understood his remoteness. As a child, Gibran

Photo by F. Holland Day, 1898

suffered from paralyzing sensitivity and existential depression, which left him withdrawn and introverted. He was protected by his mother and found comfort in his art, particularly during the intense transition from rural Lebanon to urban Boston.

p. 10   "*The sea that calls all things unto her calls me, and I must embark*": Kahlil Gibran, 97.
When Gibran was eight years old, his father's involvement in Bsharri's political upheaval cost the family everything they owned. There are varying accounts of what happened and why, but the consistent points are twofold: Gibran's mother was determined to save her family by emigrating to America, and Gibran refused to speak of this event throughout his life.

p. 14   Khalil's family arrived in Boston
After a journey of five thousand miles, Gibran's family arrived in America on June 25, 1895. Gibran was twelve years old. They spent their first night on Ellis Island, waiting to be processed by Immigration and Naturalization officials. The next day they embarked on the last leg of their journey, north to Boston, which housed the second largest Middle Eastern immigrant community in America (the largest being in New York City).

p. 14   "*Deep is your longing for the land of your memories*": Kahlil Gibran, 101.
While Kahlil's mother encouraged him to attend the Quincy School, his brother, Peter, as the eldest, was needed to run the family's store. His sisters, Sultana and Marianna, were not allowed to go to school due to what author Jean Gibran described as "the cloistered traditions of Middle Eastern women" (Jean Gibran and Kahlil Gibran, 30). Neither Sultana nor Marianna ever learned to read or write.

p. 17   like a flock of swooping birds
According to Gibran's biographer (and cousin) Jean Gibran: "Years

after he had left Boston and was studying in Paris, a flock of birds reminded Gibran of the streets where he had played, and he told a story of trying to fly a kite in a crowded South End street. He was stopped by a policeman. . . . Like thousands of other South End immigrant children, the shy, introverted country boy from the land of the Mountain adapted to his new surroundings, finding the instinct and will not only to survive but to succeed in the context of city life" (Jean Gibran and Kahlil Gibran, 32).

p. 19   *"He only bent his head; and those who stood near saw his tears falling"*: Kahlil Gibran, 101.

Gibran's life in Boston only increased his sensitivity, particularly due to the mass cultural misunderstanding of those referred to as "Syrian immigrants." The fact that his mother peddled fabric door-to-door to mansions of the Back Bay would have been looked down upon by social reformers who felt that immigrants would fare best if they assimilated to American ways. But she was undeterred, and her peddling helped her save enough money to open a small dry goods store for her family to run, elevating her family's economic security.

p. 20   a photographer named Fred Holland Day

On November 25, 1896, when Gibran was thirteen, Jessie Fremont Beale, a social worker at the Children's Aid Society, wrote to Bostonian bohemian photographer Fred Holland Day: "If you may happen to have an artist friend who would care to become interested in a little Assyrian boy. . . . He strolled into a drawing class at the College Settlement on Tyler Street last winter and showed a sufficient ability to . . . some day [earn] his living in a better way, than by selling matches or newspapers on the street. . . . I fear you will feel this request in regard to Kahlil almost an intrusion, but I am so interested in the little fellow myself, and yet so utterly helpless, that I feel as if I must try to find some one else who can be of real use to him" (quoted in Jean Gibran and Kahlil Gibran, 37–38).

Day agreed to meet Gibran, and two weeks later, they began a lifelong friendship that positioned Gibran in Boston's fine art society.

Photo by F. Holland Day, Library of Congress

p. 23   he sold his pictures to a publisher

An article in the April 2, 1898, edition of *The Critic*, a weekly New York review of fine art, describes the following scene: "Some days ago a Syrian youth no more than sixteen years of age walked into the office of Mr. S. W. Marvin of Messrs. Scribner's. He carried a letter of introduction in his hand and a portfolio of drawings under his arm. In very good English, he asked Mr. Marvin to read the one and glance over the contents of the other. Mr. Marvin did as requested. . . . The boy sat modestly by while his portfolio was being examined. It was found to contain a collection of the most striking . . . designs for book covers. When Mr. Marvin had run his critical eye over them, the boy asked him if there were any that he might find worth using. 'Have you any more?' inquired Mr. Marvin, to which the boy replied that all he had were there. 'I will take them all,' said Mr. Marvin" (quoted in Jean Gibran and Kahlil Gibran, 65). Gibran was fifteen at the time.

p. 25   *"Alone and without his nest shall the eagle fly across the sun"*: Kahlil Gibran, 98.

Gibran's mother and brother were worried by his swift Americanization and insisted that he finish his schooling in Lebanon. Gibran's mentors in Boston's fine art society threw him a farewell supper, and by September 1898, he was studying at the

Maronite college Madrasat-al-Hikmah in Beirut. While he spoke Arabic fluently and read it well, Gibran had to work hard to catch up to his peers at writing in Arabic. Similar to his experience at the Quincy School, he stood out to his teachers as "a strange boy marked by extravagances in style and attitude" (Jean Gibran and Kahlil Gibran, 77).

p. 27 *"We are the seeds of the tenacious plant, and it is in our ripeness and our fullness of heart that we are given to the wind and are scattered"*: Kahlil Gibran, 153.

"My father hurt me often," Gibran wrote in 1911, remembering his college breaks when he returned home to Bsharri and faced a commanding patriarch. At one dinner party, seventeen-year-old Gibran was begged to read a poem he'd newly written. He recalled, "It was my first reading ever to a selected audience—I cannot describe what it was to me. But they all were with me— they were loving me. And my father said—'I hope we shall never have any more of this stuff—this sick-mindedness.' That hurt deep into my inner most being" (quoted in Jean Gibran and Kahlil Gibran, 84).

Gibran soon left his father's house and lived in destitution with the same cousin who had been with him when he'd fallen and broken his shoulder all those years ago. The poverty wounded Gibran's pride, but just as he had as a child, "Kahlil found solace along the cliffs, in the gorges, and in the dark shadows of the Cedars" (Jean Gibran and Kahlil Gibran, 85).

p. 28 *"Know that all the blessed dead are standing about you and watching"*: Kahlil Gibran, 115.

The deaths of three of Gibran's four immediate family members in quick succession brought a new darkness to his life. For the first time since his youth, his art dropped away. Sultana died at the age of fourteen in April 1902 from a long illness, and although Gibran tried to make it back from Beirut in time, he missed her. Peter died of consumption in February 1903 and his mother of cancer in June the same year. Gibran was twenty. The metaphor I've used on this page—sadness as "a wall between two gardens"—is from Gibran's *Sand and Foam: A Book of Aphorisms*, New York, Knopf, 1926, 70.

p. 31 *"Work is love made visible"*: Kahlil Gibran, 115.

Gibran's life went in a new direction when Fred Holland Day arranged for an exhibition of Gibran's art at Day's own studio in the spring of 1904, advertising under the reclaimed name of Gibran Khalil Gibran. During the viewing, Gibran was introduced to Mary Elizabeth Haskell, who would become a lifelong confidant, patron, and unrequited love for Gibran.

Haskell wrote in her diary, "I told him frankly how much I used to wish people might know he loved me because it was the greatest honor I had and I wanted credit for it, wanted the fame of his loving me. He wants it known that I had faith in him and made his start possible, that I backed him financially" (quoted in Bushrui and Sammons, 19).

p. 33 *"Let there be spaces in your togetherness . . . of your souls"*: Kahlil Gibran, 105.

Haskell paid for Gibran to study art at the Academy Julian in Paris from 1908 to 1910 and afterward relocated him to New York City. Gibran's philosophic and poetic masterpiece, *The Prophet*, was published in 1923, when he was forty years old. Since its initial publication, *The Prophet* has been translated into forty languages, has never gone out of print, and has become one of the best-selling books of all time. Gibran wrote and painted for the rest of his life—only eight more years. He died in 1931 and was buried in Bsharri, where a museum stands in his memory.

*B*IBLIOGRAPHY

Bushrui, Suheil, and Tania June Sammons. *The Art of Kahlil Gibran at Telfair Museums.* Savannah, GA: Telfair Books, 2010.

Gibran, Jean, and Kahlil Gibran. *Kahlil Gibran: His Life and World.* New York: Avenel, 1981.

Gibran, Kahlil. *The Collected Works.* New York: Knopf, 2007.

UNESCO World Heritage Centre. "Ouadi Qadisha (the Holy Valley) and the Forest of the Cedars of God (Horsh Arz El-Rab)." whc.unesco.org/en/list/850.

For Situ & Jidu, with all my love
CM

To my godmother and early mentor,
Deloris Harris, Everett, MA
EK

First edition 2022

Library of Congress Catalog Card Number 2021946639
ISBN 978-1-5362-0032-4

22 23 24 25 26 27 LEO 10 9 8 7 6 5 4 3 2 1

Printed in Heshan, Guangdong, China

This book was typeset in Amiri.
The illustrations were done in collage and acrylic on paper.

Candlewick Press
99 Dover Street
Somerville, Massachusetts 02144

www.candlewick.com